Case Overview

Feldman v. Schocket (2022) is a pivotal Florida appellate case examining the tension between testamentary intent and constitutional homestead protections. The case centers on whether Jeffrey Schocket, the surviving spouse, effectively waived his homestead rights, allowing the personal representative of the estate, Robert Feldman, to sell the property as directed in the decedent's will.

Key Legal Principles

1. Homestead Protections (Article X, Section 4(c) of the Florida Constitution):

   - Homestead property cannot be freely devised if the decedent is survived by a spouse or minor children, except to the surviving spouse (if no minor children exist).

   - This provision safeguards surviving spouses and minor children from losing their home after the death of the property owner.

2. Validity of Waivers (Florida Statutes § 732.702):

   - Spousal waivers must meet strict statutory requirements, including "fair disclosure" of the estate's assets for waivers executed after marriage. Waivers cannot be effectuated posthumously.

Case Facts

- The decedent, Patricia Silver, directed in her will that the homestead property be sold and its proceeds added to her residuary estate a clear violation of Florida's constitutional homestead devise restrictions.

- The executor argued that the surviving spouse waived his homestead rights through:

  1. A Pre-Death Mortgage Waiver: Schocket signed a mortgage document that included language purporting to waive his homestead rights under Article X, Section 4(c).

  2. A Post-Death Waiver: Shortly after Silver's passing, Schocket signed another document that the executor claimed waived his rights.

Court Findings

Mortgage Waiver:

- The court ruled this waiver invalid. Though spousal signatures on mortgages are constitutionally required to alienate homestead property during the owner's life, this does not equate to a waiver of homestead rights after death.

- The court also deemed the waiver language insufficiently specific and considered it "boilerplate" wording, which courts disfavor.

Post-Death Waiver:

- The waiver was similarly invalidated because:
  - Florida law does not permit posthumous waivers of homestead rights.
  - The statutory requirement of "fair disclosure" of estate assets was not met.

Conclusion and Implications

The court upheld Schocket's homestead rights, reinforcing Florida's robust constitutional protections for surviving spouses.

This case emphasizes that:
- Waivers of homestead rights must be explicit, informed, and fully compliant with statutory requirements.
- Estate planners and testators should exercise caution and ensure their plans do not conflict with homestead protections, as these rights vest immediately upon death and cannot be waived retroactively.

For estate planning, this case serves as a cautionary tale about the limits of testamentary freedom when homestead property is involved. Proper legal advice and compliance with statutory requirements are essential to avoid unintended outcomes.

THE DECISION

FELDMAN v. SCHOCKET (2022)

District Court of Appeal of Florida, Third District.

Robert FELDMAN, etc., Appellant, v. Jeffrey SCHOCKET, Appellee.

No. 3D21-1509

Decided: September 21, 2022

Before FERNANDEZ, C.J., and EMAS, and MILLER, JJ.

Annesser Armenteros, PLLC, John W. Annesser, Islamorada, and Megan Conkey Gonzalez, for appellant. Tom Woods P.A., and Tom Woods, for appellee.

Appellant, Robert Feldman, acting in his capacity as Personal Representative of the Estate of Patricia Silver, challenges a final judgment granting appellee, Jeffrey Schocket, Silver's widower, homestead rights pursuant to a petition for declaratory relief. Silver died testate while married to Schocket. In her will, she directed that her homestead be sold and the proceeds placed in the residue for distribution along with her other assets. The trial court determined that two mortgage waivers and a spousal waiver were ineffective to override the constitutional homestead protection afforded to Schocket that otherwise prevented Silver from directing the sale of the property. Discerning no error, we affirm.

BACKGROUND

Schocket and Silver were married in 2003. During their marriage, they resided together at 208 Buttonwood Lane, Islamorada, Florida. In 2015, Silver mortgaged the Islamorada property to obtain a loan to fund her law firm, the Silver Law Firm, P.A. Schocket signed two mortgages. Both mortgages contained identical waivers, providing, in relevant part: "Mortgagor, [Schocket], is joining in the execution of this mortgage for the sole purpose of waiving his or her homestead rights under Article X, Section 4 of the Florida Constitution, and shall not be bound by the terms, conditions or warranties contained in this instrument." The mortgages were notarized, witnessed by two persons, and duly recorded.

On October 26, 2016, Silver passed away. Silver's will, executed two days before her death, provided that the Islamorada property "shall be sold by [Silver's] executor, the proceeds of which . shall become part of [Silver's] residuary estate. Until such time as the property is sold, my husband Jeffrey Schocket may reside in the property."

Schocket continued to reside at the property, and on November 17, 2016, Feldman presented him with a spousal waiver. Schocket signed the waiver in the presence of two attesting witnesses, but the document was not notarized or recorded. According to Schocket, Feldman informed him that signing the document would enable the Estate to "pay the bills to maintain the house" and allow Feldman to serve as executor. Schocket attested he "didn't read the document" and "wasn't aware of [his] rights or interest in the property at that time."

The spousal waiver provided:

I, JEFFREY SCHOCKET, herby [sic] waive, any and all right, title, and interest I have in the property . Specifically . any rights, title and/or interest that I may have to claim that the aforementioned property is exempt and/or excluded from my wife, Patricia M. Silver's estate pursuant to Florida Statute § 732.401 or Florida Statute § 732.4015.

On December 30, 2016, Feldman was appointed Personal Representative of the Estate. Although Schocket remained in possession of the property, the Estate maintained the property and satisfied all related expenses.

In September of 2017, the property sustained damage during Hurricane Irma, rendering it uninhabitable. The following month, Feldman notified Schocket he had procured a potential buyer for the property. Schocket then filed suit seeking a determination that the property was homestead property. In response, Feldman filed an answer and raised the following affirmative defenses: (1) set-off; (2) waiver; (3) laches; (4) failure to mitigate damages; and (5) estoppel.

Schocket sought summary judgment under Florida's "old" summary judgment rule. See Fla. R. Civ. P. 1.510(c) (2020) ("The judgment sought must be rendered immediately if the pleadings and summary judgment evidence on file show that there is no genuine issue as to any material fact and that the moving party is entitled to a judgment as a matter of law."). The court convened a hearing and granted the motion, in part. In the ensuing order, the court found: (1) the 2015 mortgage waivers were limited to the mortgage agreement; and (2) the 2016 spousal waiver was procedurally noncompliant and ineffective because, upon Silver's death, Schocket acquired a vested fee simple interest in the property.

Schocket subsequently filed a renewed motion under the "new" summary judgment rule, seeking to extinguish Feldman's affirmative defenses. See Fla. R. Civ. P. 1.510(a) (2022) ("The court shall grant summary judgment if the movant shows that there is no genuine dispute as to any material fact and the movant is entitled to judgment as a matter of law."); In re Amends. to Fla. Rule of Civ. Proc. 1.510, 309 So. 3d 192, 192 (Fla. 2020) (explaining transition to federal summary judgment standard, effective May 1, 2021). The trial court granted the motion, and the instant appeal ensued.

STANDARD OF REVIEW

We review a grant of summary judgment de novo. Volusia Cnty. v. Aberdeen at Ormond Beach, L.P., 760 So. 2d 126, 130 (Fla. 2000). In this case, the parameters of our review are further informed by both Florida's "old" and "new" summary judgment standards. Pursuant to the old standard, summary judgment was proper "if there [was] no genuine issue of material fact and if the moving party [was] entitled to a judgment as a matter of law." Id. In accordance with this test, "the existence of any competent evidence creating an issue of fact, however credible or incredible, substantial or trivial, stop[ped] the inquiry and preclude[d] summary judgment, so long as the 'slightest doubt' [was] raised." Bruce J. Berman & Peter D. Webster, Berman's Florida Civil Procedure § 1.510:5 (2020 ed.). Under the new standard, which mirrors its federal counterpart and aims "to improve the fairness and efficiency of Florida's civil justice system, to relieve parties from the expense and burdens of meritless litigation, and to save the work of juries for cases where there are real factual disputes that need resolution," we view the evidence through a slightly different lens. In re Amends. to Fla. Rule of Civ. Proc. 1.510, 309 So. 3d at 194; see Fla. R. Civ. P. 1.510(a) (2022). The amended rule states that summary judgment is appropriate where "there is no genuine dispute as to any material fact and the movant is entitled to judgment as a matter of law." Fla. R. Civ. P. 1.510(a) (2022). Accordingly, "the correct test for the existence of a genuine factual dispute is whether 'the evidence is such that a reasonable jury could return a verdict for the nonmoving party.' " In re Amends. to Fla. Rule of Civ. Proc. 1.510, 317 So. 3d 72, 75 (Fla. 2021) (quoting Anderson v. Liberty Lobby, Inc., 477 U.S. 242, 248, 106 S.Ct. 2505, 91 L.Ed.2d 202 (1986)). In other words, "[i]f the evidence is merely colorable, or is not significantly probative, summary judgment may be granted." Anderson, 477 U.S. at 249–50, 106 S.Ct. 2505 (citations omitted).

ANALYSIS

Resolution of this dispute is governed by a convergence of the constitutional and statutory provisions that govern the unique homestead protections afforded under Florida law. "The first appearance of homestead provisions was in the 1868 Florida Constitution, and it was intended to prevent wholesale loss of homes and farms after the conclusion of the Civil War." Tae Kelley Bronner & Rohan Kelley, Homestead and Exempt Personal Property, in Prac. Under Fla. Prob. Code § 19.3 (10th ed. 2020). Given their unique characteristics, Florida's homestead laws have been repeatedly characterized as "our legal chameleon." See generally Harold B. Crosby & George John Miller, Our Legal Chameleon, the Florida Homestead Exemption I-III, 2 U. Fla. L. Rev. 12 (1949). Homestead protection "will be given different meanings depending on the context in which it is used." S. Walls, Inc. v. Stilwell Corp., 810 So. 2d 566, 568–69 (Fla. 5th DCA 2002); see Bowers v.

Mozingo, 399 So. 2d 492, 493 (Fla. 3d DCA 1981); Willens v. Garcia, 53 So. 3d 1113, 1119 (Fla. 3d DCA 2011).

The Florida Constitution extends three distinct protections to homestead property. See art. X, § 4, Fla. Const. "First, a clause . provides homesteads with an exemption from taxes. Second, the homestead provision protects the homestead from forced sale by creditors. Third, the homestead provision delineates the restrictions a homestead owner faces when attempting to alienate or devise the homestead property." Snyder v. Davis, 699 So. 2d 999, 1001–02 (Fla. 1997) (footnotes omitted). This case involves the third protection.

Article X, section 4(c) of the Florida Constitution provides, in pertinent part:

The homestead shall not be subject to devise if the owner is survived by spouse or minor child, except the homestead may be devised to the owner's spouse if there be no minor child. The owner of homestead real estate, joined by the spouse if married, may alienate the homestead by mortgage, sale or gift and, if married, may by deed transfer the title to an estate by the entirety with the spouse.

See also § 732.401(1), Fla. Stat. (2022) ("If not devised as authorized by law and the constitution, the homestead shall descend in the same manner as other intestate property; but if the decedent is survived by a spouse and one or more descendants, the surviving spouse shall take a life estate in the homestead, with a vested remainder to the descendants in being at the time of the decedent's death per stirpes."). By preserving the homestead status of the property, this provision "is designed to protect two classes of persons[,] . surviving spouses and minor children." Wadsworth v. First Union Nat'l Bank of Fla., 564 So. 2d 634, 636 (Fla. 5th DCA 1990).

"[T]he homestead law is to be liberally construed for the benefit of the surviving spouse it was designed to protect." In re Est. of Donovan, 550 So. 2d 37, 39 (Fla. 2d DCA 1989). Consequently, ordinarily, "equitable principles cannot operate to nullify a homestead interest." Rutherford v. Gascon, 679 So. 2d 329, 331 (Fla. 2d DCA 1996). Such an interest, however, may be waived. Waiver has been recognized by both legislative enactment and judicial imprimatur. See § 732.702(1), Fla. Stat. (2022); see also City Nat'l Bank of Fla. v. Tescher, 578 So. 2d 701, 703 (Fla. 1991) ("[W]hen a decedent is survived by no minor children and the surviving spouse has waived homestead rights, there is no constitutional restriction on devising homestead property."); Hartwell v. Blasingame, 564 So. 2d 543, 545 (Fla. 2d DCA 1990) ("[W]e see no reason for the state to prohibit [the surviving spouse] from validly waiving her homestead rights at the inception of the marital relationship which invoked those rights."); In re Amend. to the Rules Regulating the Fla. Bar Rule 4-1.5(f)(4)(B) of the

Rules of Pro. Conduct, 939 So. 2d 1032, 1038 (Fla. 2006) ("Florida's highly valued constitutional homestead protection is subject to waiver.").

"In order to find that a survivor spouse has waived/relinquished homestead protection, evidence must demonstrate the survivor's intent to waive the constitutional and statutory claim to homestead property." Rutherford, 679 So. 2d at 331. In this context, waiver is statutorily circumscribed.

Section 732.702(1), Florida Statutes, authorizes a spouse to waive homestead rights "before or after marriage, by a written contract, agreement, or waiver, signed by the waiving party in the presence of two subscribing witnesses." In such circumstances, "[u]nless the waiver provides to the contrary, a waiver of 'all rights,' or equivalent language," may constitute a waiver of all homestead rights that would otherwise inure to the benefit of the waiving spouse. Id.; see also § 732.7025(1), Fla. Stat. (2022) ("A spouse waives his or her rights as a surviving spouse with respect to the devise restrictions under [section] 4(c), Art. X of the State Constitution if the following or substantially similar language is included in a deed: 'By executing or joining this deed, I intend to waive homestead rights that would otherwise prevent my spouse from devising the homestead property described in this deed to someone other than me.' "). If the waiver is executed after marriage, each spouse is additionally required to make a fair disclosure to the other of his or her estate. §

732.702(2), Fla. Stat. Notably, the statute contains no provision for effectuating waiver after death.

Section 739.104, Florida Statutes (2022), further allows a beneficiary to disclaim an interest in property. Pursuant to the statute, any disclaimer must:

(i) be in writing, (ii) declare that the writing is a disclaimer, (iii) describe the interest or power disclaimed, (iv) be signed by the person making the disclaimer, (v) be witnessed and acknowledged in the manner provided for by deeds of real estate, and (vi) be delivered in the manner provided in section 739.301 of the Florida Statutes.

Lee v. Lee, 263 So. 3d 826, 827 (Fla. 3d DCA 2019); see § 739.104(3), Fla. Stat. Like a deed, the disclaimer must further comply with chapter 695, Florida Statutes, which states:

An acknowledgment or a proof may be taken, administered, or made within this state by or before a judge, clerk, or deputy clerk of any court; a United States commissioner or magistrate; or any notary public or civil-law notary of this state, and the certificate of acknowledgment or proof must be under the seal of the court or officer, as the case may be.

§ 695.03(1), Fla. Stat. (2022). Against this background, we examine the instant case.

Here, all three waivers were executed after marriage. Yet, the undisputed evidence established that Schocket was not provided with a fair disclosure of Silver's estate. This omission runs afoul of the applicable statutory scheme. See § 732.702(2), Fla. Stat. Further, nowhere do the mortgage waivers reference the constitutional prohibition on devise in the event a decedent is survived by a spouse or minor child. Instead, by their plain language, the mortgage waivers were executed for a qualified purpose. Without Schocket's signature, the mortgages would not constitute a valid lien on the property. See Pitts v. Pastore, 561 So. 2d 297, 301 (Fla. 2d DCA 1990). Thus, his signature was necessary to facilitate the constitutionally permissible purpose of "alienat[ing] the homestead by mortgage." See art. X, § 4(c), Fla. Const.

Further, in Chames v. DeMayo, 972 So. 2d 850 (Fla. 2007), echoing the words of this court, Justice Cantero sagaciously cautioned against enforcing boilerplate homestead waivers buried within documents of other legal significance:

[T]he waiver of the homestead exemption will become an everyday part of contract language for everything from the hiring of counsel to purchasing cellular telephone services. The average citizen, who is of course charged with reading the contracts he or she signs . often fails to read or understand boilerplate language detailed in consumer purchase contracts, language which the contracts themselves often permit to be modified upon no more than notification in a monthly statement or bill. [S]uch consumers may lose their homes because of a "voluntary divestiture" of their homestead rights for nothing more than failure to pay a telephone bill. This inevitably will result in whittling away this century old constitutional exemption until it becomes little more than a distant memory.

Id. at 862 (alterations in original) (quoting DeMayo v. Chames, 30 Fla. L. Weekly D2692, D2695–96 (Fla. 3d DCA Nov. 30, 2005) (Wells, J., dissenting)). In this case, the qualified mortgage waivers were buried within documents of other legal significance. Under these circumstances, we conclude, as did the trial court, that the mortgage waivers are procedurally deficient and insufficient to "evince an intent by [Schocket] to waive [his] homestead rights." Rutherford, 679 So. 2d at 330.

Although the post-death spousal waiver contains more expansive language than the mortgage waivers, as indicated previously, it, too, fails for a myriad of reasons. First, as previously noted, despite the fact that it was executed after marriage, it was not accompanied by fair disclosure of Silver's estate. See § 732.702(2), Fla. Stat. Second, section 732.702(1), Florida Statutes, anticipates that a party will contract with "a present or prospective spouse" or in anticipation of "separation, dissolution of marriage, or divorce." The statute does not contemplate contracting with a deceased spouse. Third, in placing their imprimatur upon waiver, courts have embraced the legal fiction that a waiver executed before or during marriage is the "legal equivalent of the prior death of the [spouse]." Jacobs v. Jacobs, 633 So. 2d 30, 32 (Fla. 5th DCA 1994) (quoting Wadsworth, 564 So. 2d at 635); see also In re Slawson's Est., 41 So. 2d 324, 326 (Fla. 1949). This legal fiction removes the constitutional impediment to devising the homestead property. See Jacobs, 633 So. 2d at 32; Wadsworth, 564 So. 2d at 635. In the absence of a waiver, however, the property passes by operation of law to the surviving spouse upon the death of the decedent. See Rutherford, 679 So. 2d at 331. Here, because the mortgage waivers failed, Schocket's property interest vested upon Silver's death. Thus, the post-death spousal waiver was too little, too late.

Feldman alternatively argues that the spousal waiver should be construed as a disclaimer. This argument fails on both procedural and substantive grounds.

Critically, the waiver is not statutorily compliant. It does not purport to be a disclaimer, it was not acknowledged before "a judge, clerk, or deputy clerk of any court; a United States commissioner or magistrate; or any notary public or civil-law notary of this state," and it was not recorded. §

695.03(1), Fla. Stat.; see § 739.104(3), Fla. Stat.; § 695.26(1), Fla. Stat. (2022). The disclaimer statute makes no provision for partial compliance.

Notwithstanding these deficiencies, Feldman relies upon Youngelson v. Youngelson's Estate, 114 So. 2d 642 (Fla. 3d DCA 1959), for the proposition that the spousal waiver is enforceable under our precedent. In Youngelson, the husband and wife executed a post-nuptial agreement. Id. at 643. The wife agreed, upon her husband's death, to release "all rights and claims in and to the Estate[,] . including rights of dower . [and] homestead rights." Id. Following the death of her husband, the wife entered into a settlement agreement with the personal representative and other heirs, affirming her release of any rights in the estate. Id. Shortly thereafter, she filed a petition to void the settlement agreement and sought to have the property declared as homestead property. Id. The trial court denied relief. Id.

This court affirmed on appeal, finding that the settlement agreement was presumptively valid and could only be set aside upon a showing of fraud or overreaching. Id. at 644. With regard to relinquishing homestead protection, the court noted "that a prohibition would not be in keeping with the best interest of litigants seeking to settle estates," and, while "courts do not favor a release of homestead rights[,] . homestead rights [can] be legally dealt with by a widow in whom they have vested." Id.

Although the holding in Youngelson remains undisturbed, the instant case is distinguishable. There was no post-death settlement here, and, perhaps more importantly, long after Youngelson was decided, the legislature exercised its prerogative to enact chapter 739 of the Florida Statutes. This statute now represents the exclusive means by which an individual may disclaim an interest in property. § 739.103, Fla. Stat. (2022) ("[T]his chapter is the exclusive means by which a disclaimer may be made under Florida law."); see also Lee, 263 So. 3d at 827 ("The Florida legislature has codified the requirements for disclaimer of property in chapter 739, the Florida Uniform Disclaimer of Property Interests Act."). Consequently, Youngelson cannot serve as a conduit for reviving a statutorily noncompliant disclaimer.

Accordingly, we conclude the trial court correctly determined the waivers were insufficient to establish Schocket intended to relinquish his homestead protection. Thus, we affirm the orders under review.1

Affirmed.

FOOTNOTES

1. ☐ We find no merit to the contention that the two-year delay in the filing of the petition precludes a determination of homestead on the ground of laches, and the record supports the conclusion that the affirmative defense of set-off has been rendered moot by a post-judgment settlement agreement. We summarily affirm the decision on the remaining affirmative defenses.

MILLER, J.

The relevant portion of
THE FLORIDA CONSTITUTION

ARTICLE X, SECTION 4. Homestead; exemptions.

(a) There shall be exempt from forced sale under process of any court, and no judgment, decree or execution shall be a lien thereon, except for the payment of taxes and assessments thereon, obligations contracted for the purchase, improvement or repair thereof, or obligations contracted for house, field or other labor performed on the realty, the following property owned by a natural person:

(1) a homestead, if located outside a municipality, to the extent of one hundred sixty acres of contiguous land and improvements thereon, which shall not be reduced without the owner's consent by reason of subsequent inclusion in a municipality; or if located within a municipality, to the extent of one-half acre of contiguous land, upon which the exemption shall be limited to the residence of the owner or the owner's family;

(2) personal property to the value of one thousand dollars.

(b) These exemptions shall inure to the surviving spouse or heirs of the owner.

(c) The homestead shall not be subject to devise if the owner is survived by spouse or minor child, except the homestead may be devised to the owner's spouse if there be no minor child. The owner of homestead real estate, joined by the spouse if married, may alienate the homestead by mortgage, sale or gift and, if married, may by deed transfer the title to an estate by the entirety with the spouse. If the owner or spouse is incompetent, the method of alienation or encumbrance shall be as provided by law.

The relevant portion of
The Florida Statutes

Title XLII ESTATES AND TRUSTS

CHAPTER 732

PROBATE CODE: INTESTATE SUCCESSION AND WILLS

PART VII

CONTRACTUAL ARRANGEMENTS

RELATING TO DEATH

732.701 Agreements concerning succession.

732.702 Waiver of spousal rights.

732.7025 Waiver of homestead rights through deed.

732.703 Effect of divorce, dissolution, or invalidity of marriage on disposition of certain assets at death.

732.701 Agreements concerning succession.

(1) No agreement to make a will, to give a devise, not to revoke a will, not to revoke a devise, not to make a will, or not to make a devise shall be binding or enforceable unless the agreement is in writing and signed by the agreeing party in the presence of two attesting witnesses. Such an agreement executed by a nonresident of Florida, either before or after this law takes effect, is valid in this state if valid when executed under the laws of the state or country where the agreement was executed, whether or not the agreeing party is a Florida resident at the time of death.

(2) The execution of a joint will or mutual wills neither creates a presumption of a contract to make a will nor creates a presumption of a contract not to revoke the will or wills.
History. s. 1, ch. 74-106; s. 39, ch. 75-220; s. 55, ch. 2001-226.
Note. Created from former s. 731.051.

732.702 Waiver of spousal rights.

(1) The rights of a surviving spouse to an elective share, intestate share, pretermitted share, homestead, exempt property, family allowance, or to assert a claim under the Florida Uniform Disposition of Community Property Rights at Death Act as described in ss. 732.216-732.228, and preference in appointment as personal representative of an intestate estate or any of those rights, may be waived, wholly or partly, before or after marriage, by a written contract, agreement, or waiver, signed by the waiving party in the presence of two subscribing witnesses. The requirement of witnesses shall be applicable only to contracts, agreements, or waivers signed by Florida residents after the effective date of this law. Any contract, agreement, or waiver executed by a nonresident of Florida, either before or after this law takes effect, is valid in this state if valid when executed under the laws of the state or country where it was executed, whether or not he or she is a Florida resident at the time of death. Unless the waiver provides to the contrary, a waiver of "all rights," or equivalent language, in the property or estate of a present or prospective spouse, or a complete property settlement entered into after, or in anticipation of, separation, dissolution of marriage, or divorce, is a waiver of all rights to elective share, intestate share, pretermitted share, homestead, exempt property, family allowance, or to assert a claim under the Florida Uniform Disposition of Community Property Rights at Death Act as described in ss. 732.216-732.228, and preference in appointment as

personal representative of an intestate estate, by the waiving party in the property of the other and a renunciation by the waiving party of all benefits that would otherwise pass to the waiving party from the other by intestate succession or by the provisions of any will executed before the written contract, agreement, or waiver.

(2) Each spouse shall make a fair disclosure to the other of that spouse's estate if the agreement, contract, or waiver is executed after marriage. No disclosure shall be required for an agreement, contract, or waiver executed before marriage.

(3) No consideration other than the execution of the agreement, contract, or waiver shall be necessary to its validity, whether executed before or after marriage.

History. s. 1, ch. 74-106; s. 39, ch. 75-220; s. 14, ch. 77-87; s. 56, ch. 2001-226; s. 10, ch. 2024-238.

732.7025 Waiver of homestead rights through deed.

(1) A spouse waives his or her rights as a surviving spouse with respect to the devise restrictions under s. 4(c), Art. X of the State Constitution if the following or substantially similar language is included in a deed:

"By executing or joining this deed, I intend to waive homestead rights that would otherwise prevent my spouse from devising the homestead property described in this deed to someone other than me."

(2) The waiver language in subsection (1) may not be considered a waiver of the protection against the owner's creditor claims during the owner's lifetime and after death. Such language may not be considered a waiver of the restrictions against alienation by mortgage, sale, gift, or deed without the joinder of the owner's spouse.
History. s. 1, ch. 2018-22.

732.703 Effect of divorce, dissolution, or invalidity of marriage on disposition of certain assets at death.

(1) As used in this section, unless the context requires otherwise, the term:

(a) "Asset," when not modified by other words or phrases, means an asset described in subsection (3), except as provided in paragraph (4)(j).

(b) "Beneficiary" means any person designated in a governing instrument to receive an interest in an asset upon the death of the decedent.

(c) "Death certificate" means a certified copy of a death certificate issued by an official or agency for the place where the decedent's death occurred.

(d) "Employee benefit plan" means any funded or unfunded plan, program, or fund established by an employer to provide an employee's beneficiaries with benefits that may be payable on the employee's death.

(e) "Governing instrument" means any writing or contract governing the disposition of all or any part of an asset upon the death of the decedent.

(f) "Payor" means any person obligated to make payment of the decedent's interest in an asset upon the death of the decedent, and any other person who is in control or possession of an asset.

(g) "Primary beneficiary" means a beneficiary designated under the governing instrument to receive an interest in an asset upon the death of the decedent who is not a secondary beneficiary. A person who receives an interest in the asset upon the death of the decedent due to the death of another beneficiary prior to the decedent's death is also a primary beneficiary.

(h) "Secondary beneficiary" means a beneficiary designated under the governing instrument who will receive an interest in an asset if the designation of the primary beneficiary is revoked or otherwise cannot be given effect.

(2) A designation made by or on behalf of the decedent providing for the payment or transfer at death of an interest in an asset to or for the benefit of the decedent's former spouse is void as of the time the decedent's marriage was judicially dissolved or declared invalid by court order prior to the decedent's death, if the designation was made prior to the dissolution or court order. The decedent's interest in the asset shall pass as if the decedent's former spouse predeceased the decedent. An individual retirement account described in s. 408 or s. 408A of the Internal Revenue

Code of 1986, or an employee benefit plan, may not be treated as a trust for purposes of this section.

(3) Subsection (2) applies to the following assets in which a resident of this state has an interest at the time of the resident's death:

(a) A life insurance policy, qualified annuity, or other similar tax-deferred contract held within an employee benefit plan.

(b) An employee benefit plan.

(c) An individual retirement account described in s. 408 or s. 408A of the Internal Revenue Code of 1986, including an individual retirement annuity described in s. 408(b) of the Internal Revenue Code of 1986.

(d) A payable-on-death account.

(e) A security or other account registered in a transfer-on-death form.

(f) A life insurance policy, annuity, or other similar contract that is not held within an employee benefit plan or a tax-qualified retirement account.

(4) Subsection (2) does not apply:

(a) ☐ To the extent that controlling federal law provides otherwise;

(b) ☐ If the governing instrument is signed by the decedent, or on behalf of the decedent, after the order of dissolution or order declaring the marriage invalid and such governing instrument expressly provides that benefits will be payable to the decedent's former spouse;

(c) ☐ To the extent a will or trust governs the disposition of the assets and s. 732.507(2) or s. 736.1105 applies;

(d) ☐ If the order of dissolution or order declaring the marriage invalid requires that the decedent acquire or maintain the asset for the benefit of a former spouse or children of the marriage, payable upon the death of the decedent either outright or in trust, only if other assets of the decedent fulfilling such a requirement for the benefit of the former spouse or children of the marriage do not exist upon the death of the decedent;

(e) ☐ If, under the terms of the order of dissolution or order declaring the marriage invalid, the decedent could not have unilaterally terminated or modified the ownership of the asset, or its disposition upon the death of the decedent;

(f) ☐ If the designation of the decedent's former spouse as a beneficiary is irrevocable under applicable law;

(g) ☐ If the governing instrument is governed by the laws of a state other than this state;

(h) ☐ To an asset held in two or more names as to which the death of one co-owner vests ownership of the asset in the surviving co-owner or co-owners;

(i) ☐ If the decedent remarries the person whose interest would otherwise have been revoked under this section and the decedent and that person are married to one another at the time of the decedent's death; or

(j) ☐ To state-administered retirement plans under chapter 121.

(5) ☐ In the case of an asset described in paragraph (3)(a), paragraph (3)(b), or paragraph (3)(c), unless payment or transfer would violate a court order directed to, and served as required by law on, the payor:

(a) ☐ If the governing instrument does not explicitly specify the relationship of the beneficiary to the decedent or if the governing instrument explicitly provides that the beneficiary is not the decedent's spouse, the payor is not liable for making any payment on account of, or transferring any interest in, the asset to the beneficiary.

(b)☐ As to any portion of the asset required by the governing instrument to be paid after the decedent's death to a primary beneficiary explicitly designated in the governing instrument as the decedent's spouse:

1.☐ If the death certificate states that the decedent was married at the time of his or her death to that spouse, the payor is not liable for making a payment on account of, or for transferring an interest in, that portion of the asset to such primary beneficiary.

2.☐ If the death certificate states that the decedent was not married at the time of his or her death, or if the death certificate states that the decedent was married to a person other than the spouse designated as the primary beneficiary at the time of his or her death, the payor is not liable for making a payment on account of, or for transferring an interest in, that portion of the asset to a secondary beneficiary under the governing instrument.

3.☐ If the death certificate is silent as to the decedent's marital status at the time of his or her death, the payor is not liable for making a payment on account of, or for transferring an interest in, that portion of the asset to the primary beneficiary upon delivery to the payor of an affidavit validly executed by the primary beneficiary in substantially the following form:

STATE OF

COUNTY OF

Before me, the undersigned authority, personally appeared by the means specified herein, (type or print Affiant's name) ("Affiant"), who swore or affirmed that:

1.☐ (Type or print name of Decedent) ("Decedent") died on (type or print the date of the Decedent's death) .

2.☐ Affiant is a "primary beneficiary" as that term is defined in Section 732.703, Florida Statutes. Affiant and Decedent were married on (type or print the date of marriage) , and were legally married to one another on the date of the Decedent's death.

(Affiant)

Sworn to or affirmed before me by means of ☐ physical presence or ☐ online notarization by the affiant who ☐ is personally known to me or ☐ has produced (state type of identification) as identification this day of (month) , (year) .

(Signature of Officer)

(Print, Type, or Stamp Commissioned name of Notary Public)

4.☐ If the death certificate is silent as to the decedent's marital status at the time of his or her death, the payor is not liable for making a payment on account of, or for transferring an interest in, that portion of the asset to the secondary beneficiary upon delivery to the payor of an affidavit validly executed by the secondary beneficiary in substantially the following form:

STATE OF

COUNTY OF

Before me, the undersigned authority, personally appeared by the means specified herein, (type or print Affiant's name) ("Affiant"), who swore or affirmed that:

1.☐ (Type or print name of Decedent) ("Decedent") died on (type or print the date of the Decedent's death) .

2.☐ Affiant is a "secondary beneficiary" as that term is defined in Section 732.703, Florida Statutes. On the date of the Decedent's death, the

Decedent was not legally married to the spouse designated as the "primary beneficiary" as that term is defined in Section 732.703, Florida Statutes.

(Affiant)

Sworn to or affirmed before me by means of ☐ physical presence or ☐ online notarization by the affiant who ☐ is personally known to me or ☐ has produced (state type of identification) as identification this day of (month) , (year) .

(Signature of Officer)

(Print, Type, or Stamp Commissioned name of Notary Public)

(6)☐ In the case of an asset described in paragraph (3)(d), paragraph (3)(e), or paragraph (3)(f), the payor is not liable for making any payment on account of, or transferring any interest in, the asset to any beneficiary.

(7)☐ Subsections (5) and (6) apply notwithstanding the payor's knowledge that the person to whom the asset is transferred is different from the person who would own the interest pursuant to subsection (2).

(8) This section does not affect the ownership of an interest in an asset as between the former spouse and any other person entitled to such interest by operation of this section, the rights of any purchaser for value of any such interest, the rights of any creditor of the former spouse or any other person entitled to such interest, or the rights and duties of any insurance company, financial institution, trustee, administrator, or other third party.

(9) This section applies to all designations made by or on behalf of decedents dying on or after July 1, 2012, regardless of when the designation was made.

History. s. 1, ch. 2012-148; s. 6, ch. 2013-172; s. 7, ch. 2021-205.

www.ingramcontent.com/pod-product-compliance
Lightning Source LLC
Chambersburg PA
CBHW082258220526
45469CB00009B/3053